A Note to Parents

DK READERS is a compelling program for beginning
readers, designed in conjunction with leading literacy
experts, including Dr. Linda Gambrell, Distinguished
Professor of Education at Clemson University. Dr. Gambrell
has served as President of the National Reading Conference,
the College Reading Association, and the International
Reading Association.

Beautiful illustrations and superb full-color photographs
combine with engaging, easy-to-read stories to offer a fresh
approach to each subject in the series. Each DK READER is
guaranteed to capture a child's interest while developing his
or her reading skills, general knowledge, and love of reading.

The five levels of DK READERS are aimed at different
reading abilities, enabling you to choose the books that
are exactly right for your child:

Pre-level 1: Learning to read
Level 1: Beginning to read
Level 2: Beginning to read alone
Level 3: Reading alone
Level 4: Proficient readers

The "normal" age at which
a child begins to read
can be anywhere from
three to eight years old.
Adult participation
through the lower levels is
very helpful for providing
encouragement, discussing
storylines, and sounding
out unfamiliar words.

No matter which level you select, you can be sure that you
are helping your child learn to read, then read to learn!

LONDON, NEW YORK, MUNICH,
MELBOURNE, AND DELHI

Senior Editor Helen Murray
Editorial Assistant Ruth Amos
Senior Designer Guy Harvey
Design Assistant Elena Jarmoskaite
Pre-production Producer Siu Yin Chan
Producer David Appleyard
Managing Editor Elizabeth Dowsett
Design Manager Ron Stobbart
Art Director Lisa Lanzarini
Publishing Manager Julie Ferris
Publishing Director Simon Beecroft

Reading Consultant Linda B. Gambrell

Rovio
Approvals Editor Rollo de Walden
Senior Graphic Designer Jan Schulte-Tigges
Publishing Director Laura Nevanlinna

Hasbro
Director of Global Publishing Michael Kelly
Senior Designer Steven Lathrop
Product Development Specialist Heather Hopkins

First published in the United States in 2014
by DK Publishing
345 Hudson Street
New York, New York 10014

10 9 8 7 6 5 4 3 2 1
001–275291–Nov/14

Page design copyright © 2014 Dorling Kindersley Limited

Published in Great Britain by Dorling Kindersley Limited.

DK books are available at special discounts when
purchased in bulk for sales promotions, premiums,
fund-raising, or educational use.
For details, contact:
DK Publishing Special Markets
345 Hudson Street, New York, New York 10014
SpecialSales@dk.com

A catalog record for this book
is available from the Library of Congress.

ISBN: 978-1-4654-3397-8 (Paperback)
ISBN: 978-1-4654-3396-1 (Hardback)

Color reproduction by Alta Image, UK
Printed and bound in China by South China

Discover more at
www.dk.com

Contents

4 Welcome to Piggy Island

6 Meet the Autobirds

8 Amazing disguises

10 The Deceptihogs

12 Optimus Prime Bird

16 Bumblebee Bird

20 Grey Slam Grimlock Bird

24 Heatwave the Fire-Bot Bird

26 Supreme showdown

28 Quiz

30 Glossary

DK READERS

BEGINNING
2
TO READ ALONE

ANGRY BIRDS
TRANSFORMERS

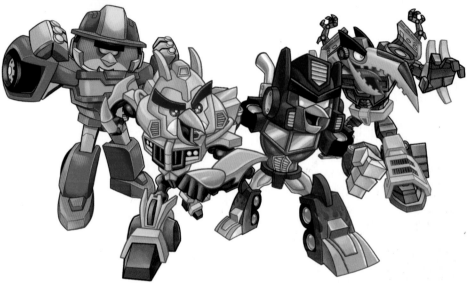

ROBOT BIRDS IN DISGUISE

Written by Helen Murray

Welcome to Piggy Island

Piggy Island may look like a beautiful paradise, but strange things have happened here lately...

A mysterious power source called the EggSpark came crashing through the sky. It turned the island's birds and pigs into robots! Even the birds' eggs grew mini legs and became Egg-bots.

The EggSpark
This is the source of all power on Piggy Island. It glows with sparks of blue energy.

Now, the Egg-bots are
changing all the plants
and rocks into robotic objects.
Piggy Island will be destroyed!

Meet the Autobirds

Squawk hello to this heroic band of robot birds!
They are called the Autobirds.
The Autobirds just want to nest in peace, but they have a very important mission.

Grey Slam
Grimlock Bird

Optimus Prime Bird

They must catch the Egg-bots
to stop them from destroying
the island.
They need to work with a team
of pig robots—the Deceptihogs.
Can the Autobirds trust the
greedy hogs and save their home?

Bumblebee Bird

Heatwave the
Fire-Bot Bird

Amazing disguises

First of all, the Autobirds must get used to their powerful new robot bodies. They have arms and legs for the first time!

Bird form

That's not all... These robots can switch form, too! They can disguise themselves as cars, trucks, and other vehicles whenever they want.

Robot form

The birds' vehicle modes are called their cyberforms.

The robot pigs can change into all kinds of awesome vehicle cyberforms, too.

Cyberform

Energon
Starscream Pig

Dark
Megatron Pig

The Deceptihogs

Attention! These pesky porkers are the Deceptihogs. They say they have united with the Autobirds, but really they will do anything they can to ruffle their feathers.

The sly robot hogs are secretly
trying to poach all the Egg-bots,
before the Autobirds find them.
The pigs plan to take them to the
leader, Dark Megatron Pig, who
dreams of gobbling eggs for
breakfast, lunch, and dinner!

Soundwave Pig

**Galvatron
Pig**

Lockdown Pig

Optimus Prime Bird

This is Optimus Prime Bird—
brave leader of the Autobirds
and protector of the Egg-bots!

Fist of
steel

Tough faceplate
Optimus's faceplate
is made of metal.
His pointed
audioreceptors
can hear even the
smallest piggy snort!

It is clear why Optimus is
top of the robot pecking order.
He is a skilled warrior and a
caring leader, too.

The Autobirds all look
up to wise Optimus.
It is not unusual for an excited
Autobird to short-circuit
when their hero is nearby!

Serious Optimus could never be called the joker of the flock. He only thinks about one thing: catching runaway Egg-bots. The Autobirds keep the Egg-bots safe so they don't destroy the island.

Large tailpipe

Fiery paintwork

Mean machine
Optimus changes into a powerful truck cyberform. It is perfect for hunting down Deceptihogs.

Optimus thought the robot pigs were helping the Autobirds, but he discovers the mischievous porkers are kidnapping Egg-bots!

He will stop the Deceptihogs. Fire up your engines: Autobirds, roll out!

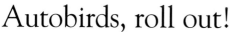

Bumblebee Bird

Who can help Optimus Prime Bird track down the Deceptihogs? Bumblebee Bird, that's who!

Bumblebee is Optimus's eager second-in-command. He was very competitive as a regular bird, but the EggSpark has scrambled his brain! Now, he just wants to be liked.

Bumblebee is always ready for action, but he often drives headfirst into danger without thinking.

Robotic rock

Piercing
blue optics

Afterburners

No bird knows why Bumblebee only communicates with his radio, rather than squawking.

Speedy Bumblebee can make quick getaways with his lightning-fast afterburners.

Unused vocal processor in beak

Hidden strength
Bumblebee's
chassis may
not be heavy
but it is
incredibly strong.

Or, he can simply turn into his
cyberform: a flashy sports car.

The Deceptihogs need to
keep their optics peeled to spot
Bumblebee Bird.
He is a blur as he zooms
around the whole island
in astroseconds.

Striped chassis

Grey Slam Grimlock Bird

Stomp, stomp, stomp... Grey Slam Grimlock Bird is close by! He is a large and powerful robotic dinosaur.

Huge foot

Grimlock Bird may be strong,
but he is very, very clumsy.
He often trips over his own feet.

This dinosaur is a mysterious
robot and does not squawk much,
but he does moan about being
nagged by Optimus.

Sharp weapon
Watch out!
Grimlock Bird's
jagged beak can
crunch straight
through the
toughest metal.

Wide central tire

Grimlock Bird will always
follow Optimus, though.
In fact, this loyal fighter
follows his leader so closely,
he pokes him with his long
beak! Oops!
There is more to Grimlock
Bird than meets the beak.
He is a strong and cunning
fighter, especially when
he converts into a
motorized trike.
He whizzes past the Deceptihogs
and uses his beak to knock them off
their robotic hooves!

Heatwave the Fire-Bot Bird

Huge Heatwave the Fire-Bot Bird is not a dainty chick—in fact, he is a hulking lump of metal!

He is a rescue worker known as a fire-bot. His cyberform is a large scarlet fire truck.

Firefighter's helmet

Strong but silent
No Autobird ever hears Heatwave squawk. He just stares and stares and stares— especially when a robot cracks a joke!

Heatwave is always first on the scene if an engine overheats.

His strong truck is great for smashing into Deceptihog vehicles head on.

The pig robots will suffer a major frag and collapse in a nano-klik!

Supreme showdown

Optimus Prime Bird is gearing up for a mighty battle!
It is time to stop the pigs poaching the Egg-bots once and for all.
Megatron tries to shoot Optimus, but he rams into the pig's side.

The wicked porker has a tantrum, and Optimus wins the battle!

The Autobirds have saved the Egg-bots from the pigs—for now! But can they catch the Egg-bots before they all wreck Piggy Island?

Quiz

1. What do the Egg-bots turn the plants and rocks into?

2. What color does the EggSpark glow?

3. Which member of the Deceptihogs is this?

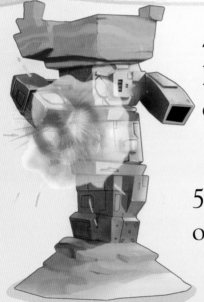

4. What does Dark Megatron Pig want to do with the Egg-bots?

5. Who is the leader of the Autobirds?

6. What color is
Bumblebee Bird?

7. Which Autobird
has a light but very
strong chassis?

8. Which Autobird
is very clumsy?

9. What vehicle does Grey Slam
Grimlock Bird turn into?

10. What color is Heatwave
the Fire-Bot Bird's truck?

1. Robotic objects, 2. Blue, 3. Dark Megatron Pig, 4. Eat them, 5. Optimus Prime Bird,
6. Yellow, 7. Bumblebee Bird, 8. Grey Slam Grimlock Bird, 9. A trike, 10. Red.

Glossary

afterburners fiery boosters that increase a robot's speed

astrosecond a short amount of time

audioreceptors a robot's ears

chassis a robot's body

communicates shares information like thoughts, feelings, and ideas with others

cunning tricky or smart

faceplate a covering that protects a robot's face

frag an error in a robot's system

mischievous bad or causing trouble

nano-klik a short amount of time

optics a robot's eyes

poach steal

short-circuit when electricity stops flowing properly

vocal processor a robot's voice

Index

afterburners 17,
18

audioreceptors 13

Autobirds 6–7, 8,
10, 11, 12, 13,
14–15, 27

Bumblebee Bird 7,
16–19

chassis 19

cyberform 9, 15,
19, 24

Dark Megatron
Pig 10, 11,
26–27

Deceptihogs 7,
10–11, 15, 16,
19, 23, 25

Egg-bots 4, 5, 7,
11, 12, 14–15,
26, 27

EggSpark 4, 16

Energon
Starscream Pig
10

faceplate 13

frag 25

Galvatron Pig 11

Grey Slam
Grimlock Bird
6, 20–23

Heatwave the
Fire-Bot Bird 7,
24–25

Lockdown Pig 11

optics 17, 19

Optimus Prime
Bird 6, 12–15,
16, 21, 23, 26–27

Piggy Island 4–5,
7, 27

Soundwave Pig 11

Here are some other DK Readers you might enjoy.

Level 2

Angry Birds™ *Star Wars*® II: Path to the Pork Side
Can Redkin Skywalker resist the power of the Pork Side?
Join the young Jedi Bird on his journey!

Angry Birds™ *Star Wars*®: Lard Vader's Villains
Meet Lard Vader and the Empire Pigs
as they try to take control of the galaxy.

The LEGO® Movie: Awesome Adventures
Meet Emmet and join him on his extraordinary
quest to save the universe.

Level 3

LEGO® Legends of Chima™: Heroes' Quest
Join the heroes of Chima™ as they set out on
a dangerous mission to save their land.

Star Wars® The Legendary Yoda
Yoda is a famous and wise Jedi. Learn all about
his legendary battles and how he uses the Force.

LEGO® Hero Factory: The Brain Wars
It's heroes vs. evil Brains when mind-controlled
beasts invade Makuhero City.